AF278357

MAYFIELD

POEMS

DENNIS RUSH

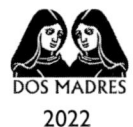

DOS MADRES

2022

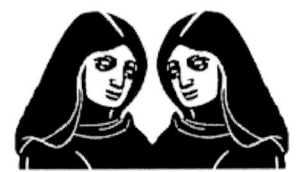

DOS MADRES PRESS INC.
P.O. Box 294, Loveland, Ohio 45140
www.dosmadres.com   editor@dosmadres.com

Dos Madres is dedicated to the belief that the small press is essential to the vitality of contemporary literature as a carrier of the new voice, as well as the older, sometimes forgotten voices of the past. And in an ever more virtual world, to the creation of fine books pleasing to the eye and hand.

Dos Madres is named in honor of Vera Murphy and Libbie Hughes, the "Dos Madres" whose contributions have made this press possible.

Dos Madres Press, Inc. is an Ohio Not For Profit Corporation and a 501 (c) (3) qualified public charity. Contributions are tax deductible.

Executive Editor: Robert J. Murphy

Illustration & Book Design: Elizabeth H. Murphy
www.illusionstudios.net

Typeset in Adobe Garamond Pro & Avenir Book
ISBN 978-1-953252-59-3
Library of Congress Control Number: 2022935619

MAYFIELD

This book is dedicated
to all who suffered:
in the path
and in the heart,
both living and dead.

TABLE OF CONTENTS

The Approaching Storm .1
Getting Close 2
Second Guessing Myself 3
Life Wasn't Going as Planned. 4
Our Hotel 5
Returning 6
The News 7
Looking for a Way to Volunteer 8
The Lady at the Check-in Table. 9
Downtown 10
The Emptiness. 11
3 Minutes. 3 Hours. .12
The Soul of a Tornado 13
Cruising Altitude 14
Surreal. 15
Domestic Violence .16
Maître d' 17
Breath 18
Hush a Bye Baby. 19
Our Hotel 20
I'm not in Charge 21
Clear Paths 22
Opportunists. 23
Renters 24
Santa 25
The End of the Day. 26
Our Hotel 27
Proverbs 22:9 28
Acceptance 29
Clothes Donations .30

The Barber 31
No Smoking 32
Managing the Floor. 33
A Couple Came In 34
The Couple Came Back. 35
Tesla Dustpan 36
Names on Duct Tape 38
How to Properly Place a Volunteer 39
Kentucky Sunrise 40
The Farmer 41
Hotel Soap 42
At the Hotel 43
Church 44
Reflection 45

About the Author 47

You could almost pause
and breathe out for a while
before being crushed.

From "Loneliness" by Tomas Tranströmer

THE APPROACHING STORM

It appears supernatural
the way dogs and cows
seem to know what is about to happen,
well before the sky turns slate gray.
Is it the atmospheric pressure?
Is it the direction of the wind?
Is it the vibrations in the ground they feel
through their hooves and paws like placing
an ear on a track to hear the rumble
minutes before you see the train?
For us, it is when a silver maple
turns its leaves upside down,
or the way the air
smells like a freshly cut pear
or the green hull of a walnut.
We detect those things too late,
and instead of running for shelter,
we stand in our yards
basking in the strange comfort
of a warm, humid breeze.
I hope the birds had a way of knowing.
I hope the squirrels knew
to come down from their nests.

GETTING CLOSE

As a child, I trained
to be a knight,
whacking down weeds
with a tobacco stick
creating ragged, unclean breaks;
mostly folding the weeds over.
That is what I see in the trees
outside of Dawson Springs
an hour away from Mayfield:
unclean breaks, things folded over.
Barns kicked down
and stomped on.

SECOND GUESSING MYSELF

Eighteen hours of driving.
Stopping for gas.
Stopping at rest stops.
A nap or two.
Plenty of time to think
and second guess myself.
I pictured an army of volunteers when I arrive.
What if this is silly? What if
they have nothing for me to do?
Surely there is something.
I warn the kids that we may be picking up trash
on the side of the highway on our own.
My daughter says we could have done that at home.

LIFE WASN'T GOING AS PLANNED.

I had that in common with Mayfield.
Near the end of the drive
a friend called and with good intentions
asked if going to a traumatized area
was what the children and I needed at this time.
I couldn't find an adequate reply.

It felt so right, I hadn't prepared myself
for justifying it to others.

OUR HOTEL

It's a dump.
$55 a night. It smells of pot.
But it's nice to not be in a car.
And, it's convenient to back the car up to the door
and clean out the garbage from the trip:
chip bags, burger wrappers and empty plastic bottles.

Thankfully, the room has a hot shower.

I put the air conditioning on to freshen the room.
The fan sounds like running a vacuum cleaner
over a gravel driveway.

RETURNING

I would have hesitated, –
paused, from driving down
without much thought,
if not for burying my father
back in November.
His death gave me permission
to care for my heritage again,
without it being about him –
his stories, his history.
He would no longer
ask me to visit someone in order
to repair a neglected friendship
on his behalf.
It was about me now.
With him gone,
home was all mine.

THE NEWS

The morning after the tornado
the news was about the destruction,
and the estimated number of dead
and the collapse of the candle factory.
And, there was also talk about global warming
as if this tragedy was somehow deserved.

LOOKING FOR A WAY TO VOLUNTEER

On the morning of the second day
we woke up at 7:00 a.m. and started driving
toward the center of town. No plan.
On the way I saw a state police station.
I stopped and asked for help finding work.
They weren't sure. They called around.
I waited. The kids were waiting in the car.

This was my fear.
I wasn't needed.
There wasn't anything for a stranger
with two children to do.

A man behind a Plexiglas window handed me a piece of paper.
It had on it the names of churches.
Then, as I was driving away,
the man behind the Plexiglas ran out of the police station
and flagged me down yelling,
"Go to the fairgrounds! Go to the fairgrounds!"

THE LADY AT THE CHECK-IN TABLE

She had a way of winking when she talked
that only a southern lady could get away with.
It implied, "If you know what I mean."
A wink to let me know what she said
was more polite than what she meant. Such as:
"This man needs help." <wink> means,
"This man is dimwitted and confused."
Or, "Can you please stay with this lady?" <wink> means,
"She looks like she's going to take more than she needs."

DOWNTOWN

is a soundless landscape
with tremendous evidence of noise.

The streets are open mouths
lined with jagged teeth.

I find it difficult to walk
through the scattered debris
of people's belongings.

There is nowhere comfortable
to rest my eyes.

Below every pile of bricks
I expect to see a lifeless human hand
reaching out.

THE EMPTINESS

Like a battleground
littered with wagon wheels and bloated horses,
this town has toppled cars
and tractor trailer trucks lying on their sides.
Buildings are gone.
I don't need to know what was here
to know what is missing.
The emptiness
is in the shape of things.

3 MINUTES. 3 HOURS

The tornado was one mile wide
and traveled 60 miles an hour.
Therefore, it only took one minute
to level one square mile.
It took 3 minutes to cross Mayfield.
It traveled 165 miles, scratching a scar
through farms and small towns.
That is the same distance
as from New York City
through Philadelphia
to Baltimore.
That trip takes 3 hours.

THE SOUL OF A TORNADO

It confuses the mind
to see destruction without reason.
Without anger.
It looks evil, but there is no evil here.
It's unfair, but unfairness is not evil.

Don't try to put a soul into a tornado,
and do not place Satan within it,
and do not say that it was missing a soul
as if to imply it should have had one.

CRUISING ALTITUDE

Where did you go, Mayfield?
The rubble doesn't add up
to what is missing.
Radar showed large amounts of debris
30,000 feet high.
So, on a clear day,
when I see a silent, silver speck
flying above me,
that is how high Mayfield went.
That's how high people's possessions went.
6.5 miles up and then fell fast and slow
miles away in fields and in trees
and caught by barbed wire fences.

SURREAL

Surreal is an overused word.
That is why it can no longer do justice
for describing an inverted world
with inverted colors
and where everything
you thought was unmovable
has been moved.

DOMESTIC VIOLENCE

Beaten, cut and bleeding.
It was a private argument.

I was intruding.
This wasn't my business.

I'm sorry I am here uninvited.
I walked in on you.
The door blown from its hinges
doesn't give me permission to treat it
like an open door.

MAÎTRE D'

I am looking at a large tree
that only has one remaining limb
bent upward at the elbow and
broken at the wrist.
It looks like a saguaro cactus
holding a wilted sheet of metal roofing
in the crook of its arm.

BREATH

I walked to the courthouse
and saw the flowers and the faces
of the dead and missing.

I couldn't catch my breath completely –
my air left in small involuntary exhales
that I couldn't replace.

It could have been crying.
A crying that stays within the chest.

HUSH A BYE BABY

Three souls in a tub,
and who do you think they be?
The mommy, the daddy, and the baby,
all of them waiting to see.
Hush little baby – it's only the wind.
Mommy's going to hold you until it ends.
There goes the butcher.
There goes the baker.
Blessed be the baby
and the candlestick maker.

OUR HOTEL

Metropolis, Illinois.

The hotel was empty.
The parking lot was empty.
The indoor pool was too cold.
It was a night of feeling too far away.

I'M NOT IN CHARGE

A lady asked me how I got to be in charge.
I said that I showed up early a couple of days in a row.
For two weeks, people arriving after me
asked me what they should do.

It wasn't complicated.
I put people where there were no people.
I told them to pick up something that was out of place
and put it in its proper place.
If someone asked me a question,
I did my best to answer.

Mostly,
I showed up often
and was early.

CLEAR PATHS

The pure products of America
should move linearly
from the trucks to
the center of the warehouse, where,
like the spoke of a wheel,
beans go to beans,
and bleach goes in the opposite direction to bleach,
and all the goods emit outwardly
from the center to their assigned locations,
ready to be carted out to the floor when needed.
We must have clear paths.
The health of this entire operation
depends upon
clear paths.

OPPORTUNISTS

There were rumors
that some people
were taking the free stuff
and going somewhere to sell it.
I'm not sure if that was true or imagined.
I did see two boys trying to take 5 shovels,
but they kindly gave back three
when we explained the reason for having limits.
They didn't seem like opportunists.

There were always rumors
of people stealing things
that were meant to be taken
for free.

RENTERS

Many of the houses in the path of the tornado
were the homes of poor uninsured renters.
Their possessions are spread across the county
and are being collected into burn piles by farmers.
If they have anything left, it's wet from not having a roof.
Their food is spoiled from not having electricity.
Their cars are damaged from trees falling on them
or being flipped across the yard.
There isn't a check in the mail for them.

SANTA

An old man
with a gray face of sadness
pressed like a cookie
into the shape of a smile
came in like a vaguely familiar celebrity
wearing a Santa suit
and holding a handful of candy canes.
He sat in a metal folding chair
and tried to cheer up the kids,
but they kept walking by.

THE END OF THE DAY

Each day, as we were leaving,
my children and I would get a small bag
and browse the isles for treats for the hotel:
cereal bars, plastic forks, paper plates
and cans of mandarin oranges.

It felt like a friend
sending us home with leftovers
after we had helped paint a room.

OUR HOTEL

I can't afford this every night:
a room that doesn't smell like anything.
Everything looks new.
The girl at the front desk
dressed professionally
with nice posture.
Live it up kids, and please,
don't leave your uncapped markers
on these crisp, white sheets.

PROVERBS 22:9

The church ladies
had a food tent
for anyone –
victims or volunteers.
Their kind faces
were there every day.
Once, they had
grilled cheese
sandwiches
on Texas toast
with a side cup
of thick
hot
tomato
soup -
not from a can –
thick and creamy.

ACCEPTANCE

A week after the tornado,
while people were still rummaging
and patching roofs, it rained hard for two days.
People came into the center looking for tarps.
They were trying to save whatever they could.
There was more lightning and high winds.
After the rain, they asked for mops.

They were so calm.
They calmly came in soaked and asked for tarps.
They calmly asked for mops.

CLOTHES DONATIONS

Frustrated truckers were turned away
at least three times after driving
a thousand miles before
they ended up here where
someone told them to unload
the truckloads of black garbage bags
full of donated clothes
into an open field.

"Let's hope it doesn't rain too hard."

We don't have the space
or the people to sort it.
None of it will be worn
by people here.

THE BARBER

He came from South Carolina
with a real barber chair
and offered free haircuts
to anyone who wanted one.
My son and I took him up on it.
"Haircuts aren't on the minds of victims." He said.
"I should have waited a week or two."
He left after a couple of slow days.

NO SMOKING

Inspectors came by.
They said we need to put up no smoking signs by the
generators.
We don't have any no smoking signs.

Occasionally, someone with a clipboard
walks around and it's assumed they are official.
However, unless they improve something
or pick up a box and help
they are mostly ignored.

Volunteering is empowering.
Here, you can choose to only pay attention
to those you trust.

MANAGING THE FLOOR

We don't need more water.
We don't take clothes here.
The ladies on the floor
are screaming for more body wash.

"What do we do with these clothes
that were dumped here last night?"

"Put them in the back left corner,
and I'll see if anyone can come take it away."

Every day is a new staff.
Every morning someone new is in charge.
We wait at the entrance at 8:00 a.m.
to see if we will have any volunteers at all.

A COUPLE CAME IN

The woman sat on the floor,
right in the middle of the aisle,
saying she was "low on sugar"
and needed a sweet drink.
She looked a mess:
A grimacing Buddha
sitting crisscross applesauce
in tight sweat pants.
Her face squished permanently
into a look of pain.
Her husband didn't care too much.
He hollered for the truck keys.
She wiggled and squeezed
her hand in her pocket, pulled out the keys
and threw them at him.
I helped her up
and carried her heavy box of groceries
out to a red truck backed up to the door.
(No one else did that). They had so much stuff.
More than they should have taken in this situation.
I struggled to get the box in the bed.
When he went to drive off, he was still in reverse
and backed into his old lady a little.
She screamed curses at him and asked me,
"Can you believe he was a truck driver?"

THE COUPLE CAME BACK

Three hours later.
They had changed shirts
as if it were a clever disguise.
Grinning possums pretending.
Someone recognized them
and said they had already gotten a fair allotment.
The guy tried to argue back
and kept walking.
He kept collecting more things.
Some people will be that way.
You have to let it go.
We don't have the manpower to clamp down.
It's not worth what we would save.

"The good will outweigh the bad,"
someone said.

TESLA DUSTPAN

Some well-meaning person was contracted
by a cutting edge company
to put together emergency kits.

Within the boxes are:
razors, shaving cream, toothpaste,
anti-bacterial wipes and Band-Aids.
There are also some odd things:
latex gloves, a dustpan
but no brush, a can of beans
but no can opener, and
sample size feminine products.

Here is the issue:
no one wants the kits
that may only contain
one or two things they need.

They don't have the room
for un-needed things,
and they don't want
to throw out what they don't need.

I have helped people load their cars
where everything they own is crammed inside:
the family, the dog, blankets, pillows and food.
There is no room
for a Tesla dustpan.

NAMES ON DUCT TAPE

Everyone is so grateful -
grateful for the donations,
grateful for anyone
who shows up to volunteer
and especially grateful
for those who keep coming back.

Volunteers show up anonymously
and never want recognition for being here.
We wouldn't know their names
if not for a required strip of duct tape on their chests
with their first name written in sharpie.

HOW TO PROPERLY PLACE A VOLUNTEER

Trust your natural prejudices.
Put the old ladies on the aisles.
      They will keep them orderly.
Old men can do security.
      Put them by the doors.
      If they can get around well,
      have them supervise the loading docks.
Young boys can carry things
      and collect trash.
Young girls can sort food.
Mothers with children can sort food.
Strong young men can unload trucks.
      They can push and pull pallet jacks.
Serious young women
      should be put in charge
      of anything important.

KENTUCKY SUNRISE

It must be the way
Great Plains dust collects and collides
with the Gulf's humidity
that has given me this morning's sunrise:
a crude Caesarian birth of a new day,
mirrored within a waveless lake.
A day with all of the potential
to overcome my fictitious,
self imposed restrictions.

THE FARMER

He looked unsure of himself, uncomfortable,
and his is overalls and denim hat were out of place
among the cans of soup and women.

Let me help you with that box.

HOTEL SOAP

Some people get bent out of shape
when they see someone
take more than is reasonable.
I don't let it get to me.
I take the small soaps from our hotel rooms
for no good reason.
I understand how it make sense
at certain times
to take a little extra
when you've never had
a little extra.

AT THE HOTEL

A truck driver
as big as a door
walked his dog
like a teardrop.

I asked him
where he called home.
He said, "Nowhere."

CHURCH

Sundays have the fewest volunteers, –
the day suffering takes a rest.
That's understandable;
the good Samaritan parable
is easy to misinterpret.
The definition of neighbor
can be ambiguous. And, it's unfair
that so many sainthoods are given
to those with empty calendars.
I'm playing the long game. Infinity
will help make this life no more
than one night in a bad hotel.
So, hang in there, unfortunate friends.
Tomorrow is just around
the corner.

REFLECTION

I'm back home
making scrambled eggs,
folding in shredded cheddar cheese
in a new pan
which makes all the difference.
I sit at my table,
eat my eggs
and watch birds
eat from their feeders.
It's quiet,
and I feel
like I have
nothing
to do.

About the Author

DENNIS RUSH grew up on a remote tobacco farm in Kentucky. He is a graduate of the University of Nebraska at Omaha and the Goddard College MFA in Creative Writing. He lives in Staatsburg, New York and is the author of *What Are the Rich Doing Tonight?*, published by Dos Madres Press in 2022.

Other books by Dennis Rush
published by Dos Madres Press

What Are The Rich Doing Tonight? (2022)

For the full Dos Madres Press catalog:
www.dosmadres.com